W9-ABJ-435

COLERIDGE'S POEMS

Coleridge's Poems

A FACSIMILE REPRODUCTION OF THE PROOFS

AND MSS. OF SOME OF THE POEMS

EDITED BY THE LATE

JAMES DYKES CAMPBELL

Author of "Samuel Taylor Coleridge, A Narrative of the Events of his Life;" and Editor of "The Poetical Works of Samuel Taylor Coleridge."

WITH PREFACE AND NOTES BY

W. HALE WHITE

WESTMINSTER

ARCHIBALD CONSTABLE AND CO.

FOLCROFT LIBRARY EDITIONS / 1972

Library of Congress Cataloging in Publication Data

Coleridge, Samuel Taylor, 1772-1834.
Coleridge's Poems.

A type facsimile prepared by Mr. Campbell before his death, from proofs owned by Mr. Potts, and a MS. in the British Museum. It includes revised proofs, interleaved with MS. of portions of the Poems of 1797, and "Ode to the departing year"; two early drafts of "The dark ladie," reprinted as "Love," and an early version of "Lewti".

I. Campbell, James Dykes, 1838-1895, ed.
PR4478.A1 1972 821'.7 72-5259
ISBN 0-8414-0020-2 (lib. bdg.)

CHISWICK PRESS:—CHARLES WHITTINGHAM AND CO.
TOOKS COURT, CHANCERY LANE, LONDON.

The number of copies of this Work which are printed for sale is limited to 250 of the small paper and 50 of the large paper editions. The latter are numbered.

PREFACE.

In his edition of Coleridge's Poetical Works (1893) Mr. Dykes Campbell says (p. 613), "There is a much-tortured draft of *Love* in the British Museum, of which (and of several other curiosities of the kind) I have printed a type-facsimile. The little volume only awaits a preface and notes." There are also other allusions to the contents of this volume in the notes to the *Poetical Works*. Mr. Campbell died soon after the printing of the facsimile was completed, and the preface and notes to it were not written. He indicated the source whence the latter part of his facsimile was derived, but there was nothing in it to show where or what was the original of the first part. At last, after much search, it was discovered to be the collection of proofs belonging to Mr. R. A. Potts, to which there is a reference at p. 574 *P. W.* Mr. Campbell had spent much labour and time upon these "curiosities," and although it can hardly be hoped that their sale will be large, it has been thought worth while to publish them. They were already printed, and there may be a few students and lovers of Coleridge to whom any record of his ways and methods may be precious. They are also evidence, although no additional evidence is needed, of the religious care with which Mr. Campbell discharged his duty as biographer and editor. I cannot attempt to supply a substitute for what he left undone. I should fear the comparison between anything I might venture to say and conjectures of what my friend would have said, and I must confine myself to a few words of description and explanation.

Mr. Potts has kindly lent me his little volume. It is bound in boards and the corrections are in Coleridge's own hand. On the back is written "Coleridge's MSS. Corrected copy of a work." On the side in Coleridge's hand are the words "Mr. Cottle's." In part it is a copy of the *Poems* of 1796 prepared for the printer, but it is not a final revise. It is interleaved in MS., and in addition to a portion of the text of 1796 it contains proofs of the notes of 1797 and of the *Ode to the Departing Year*. The 1796 text in the present reprint is on white paper. The MS·

interleaving and the proofs of notes are on blue paper. The proofs of the *Ode* are on white paper. Erased letters, words and passages, are printed in italics and are enclosed in brackets. The paging of the reprint is at the bottom.

Advertisement.—This is to be found at p. 243 of the *Poems* of 1797. The list of poems following the advertisement is the list of Coleridge's poems in the supplement to that edition excluding *On the Christening of a Friend's Child.*

Religious Musings (p. 55).—The passage about Priestley which is here struck out was restored in 1797, but without the two and a half lines beginning at "Whom that" expressing "impotent regret" that the author had never seen him.

Notes.—There are three sets of proofs of the notes which follow those on *Religious Musings*, but the first ends in the middle of note 13 about light from plants. The third proof is uncorrected. There is also an uncorrected proof of the note on the Chatterton Monody. Mr. Campbell has printed only one set incorporating in it all the corrections with the exception of one or two which are of no importance.

Note on the Monody to Chatterton.—This is the suppressed note to which Cottle refers (*Early Recollections*, i. 34—*Reminiscences*, 24). He says, "on this note being shown to me, I remarked that 'Captain Blake, whom he occasionally met, was the son-in-law of Dean Milles.' 'What,' said Mr. Coleridge, 'the man with the great sword?' 'The same,' I answered. 'Then,' said Mr. C. with an assumed gravity, 'I will suppress this note to Chatterton; the fellow might have my head off before I am aware!' To be sure there was something rather formidable in his huge dragoon's sword, constantly rattling by his side! This Captain Blake was a member of the Bristol Corporation, and a pleasant man, but his sword was prodigious! 'The sight of it,' Mr. C. said, 'was enough to set half-a-dozen poets scampering up Parnassus, as though hunted by a wild mastadon.'" Cottle then professes to give the note, but his version differs from that of the MS. now printed.

Note to the Sonnet on Burke.—The cancelled passage is taken from the *Watchman*, No. i. p. 22, (See *P. W.*, p. 574). The last paragraph of the note seems to assume the existence of the *Watchman*, and it may have been actually written before 13 May, 1796, when the *Watchman* came to an end, although the proof is set up for the edition of 1797.

Note to The Composition of a Kiss.—Mr. E. R. Norris Mathews, the City Librarian at Bristol, has kindly given me the following description of the *Carmina Quadragesimalia* to which Coleridge refers.

[The title-page: vol. i.] Carmina | quadragesimalia | ab | ædis Christi | Oxon. | Alumnis composita | et ab | ejusdem ædis | Baccalaureis Determinantibus | in | Schola | Naturalis Philosophiæ | publice recitata.

Oxonii, | e Theatro Sheldoniano | MDCCXXIII. |

[The title page of the second volume is identical as far as "recitata," then—] Volumen Secundum. | Oxonii, e Theatro Sheldoniano, | MDCCXLVIII.

Coleridge alters "Adiddit" (*sic*) to "Addit et," but it is "Additit" in the original. Who "L. Thomas" was is not known. The title of the poem is "An Omne Corpus Componatur? Affr."

Ode on the Departing Year.—There are two proofs, neither of them final revises, but the second comes after the first in order of time. This is evident from Coleridge's remark at p. 97 and Cottle's reply at p. 111. Cottle and his printer have therefore paid but small attention to Coleridge's directions, and Cottle's note on the second proof to the line *In the black chamber, etc.*, is wrong, as it is clearly struck out in the first proof. The reference on p. 88 is to Bishop Lowth's *Short Introduction to English Grammar.* The list of poems (p. 98) is a list of all Charles Lloyd's poems included in the edition of 1797.

The remainder of Mr. Campbell's facsimile consists of extracts from the British Museum MSS. quoted on p. 113. They are bound in a thin volume, which was bought of Mr. H. Bohn in 1868. It contains *To Lesbia, Morienti Superstes, The Death of the Starling*, three lines from *Dejection*, and a prose note besides the poems now printed. The leaves are separate and belong to different dates.

The Dark Ladie.—This was first printed in the *Morning Post* of 21 Dec., 1799. It next appeared, greatly altered, as *Love*, in the second (1800) edition of the *Lyrical Ballads*. There are four forms of it known to me, that of the present transcript, the *Morning Post*, the Longman MS.,[1] and the *Lyrical Ballads*. It would be interesting to print a variorum edition of the poem, but as this is impossible in the space allotted to me, reference must be made by the reader who wishes to understand the relationship between these four forms to *P. W.*, pp. 612-614. The MS. of our facsimile is clearly prior to the *Morning Post*. The two stanzas following the fifth to the left and right are essays in the construction of two stanzas in the *Morning Post*. The last line of the 28th stanza is to be found in a remodelled stanza in the *Post* and in the Longman MS., but Coleridge has obliterated the whole verse in the latter. This is enough to show, independently of all the other obvious considerations, that it is an early, if not the first draft, which we have before us. The exquisite 25th stanza has not before

[1] *A Description of the Wordsworth and Coleridge MSS. in the possession of Mr. T. Norton Longman.* Edited with notes by W. Hale White, 1897.

been printed. To my mind and ear it is inimitable, and it is of itself sufficient to justify the publication of Mr. Campbell's labours.

The second MS. is an incomplete copy of *Love.* Those stanzas which are found in the MS. vary but slightly from those in the final version, with the exception of the last two on p. 127. The first of these is in the *Post* and Longman MSS., but, as I have just said, has been struck out in the latter, and is consequently not in the *Lyrical Ballads.* The second of the two stanzas corresponds with the *Post* and Longman MSS. The date of this portion of the MS. of the facsimile is probably after that of the *Post* and before that of the Longman MSS.

Lewti.—It may be worth while to note that Coleridge most likely takes his "Tamaha" from the "Alatamaha" of Bartlett's *Travels in North America* (p. 12).

W. HALE WHITE.

MS. IN THE POSSESSION OF MR. POTTS.

[MS.]

ADVERTISEMENT.

N.B. To be placed before the poems which I have retained.

[MS.]

ADVERTISEMENT.

I HAVE excepted the following Poems from thoſe, which I had determined to omit. Some intelligent friends particularly requeſted it, obſerving, that what moſt delighted me, when I was "young in *writing* poetry, would probably beſt pleaſe thoſe, who are young in *reading* poetry: and a man muſt learn to be *pleaſed* with a ſubject before he can yield [*give*] that attention to it, which is requiſite in order to acquire a juſt taſte." I however was fully convinced, that he, who gives to the Preſs what he does not thoroughly approve in his own cloſet, commits an act of diſreſpect [*or*] both againſt himſelf and his fellow-citizens. The requeſt & the reaſoning would not therefore have influenced me, had they not been aſſiſted by other motives. The firſt in order of theſe Verſes, which I have thus endeavoured to *reprieve* from immediate oblivion, was originally addreſſed "To the Author of Poems publiſhed anonymouſly, at Briſtol." A ſecond Edition of theſe poems has lately appeared with the Author's name prefixed, and I could not refuſe myſelf the gratification of ſeeing the name of that man among my poems, without whoſe kindneſs they would probably have remained unpubliſhed; and to whom I know myſelf greatly & variouſly obliged, as a poet, a man, and a Chriſtian.—The ſecond is entitled "an Effuſion on an autumnal Evening, written in early youth." In a note to this poem I had aſſerted, that the Tale of Florio in Mr Rogers's "Pleaſures of Memory" was to be found in the Loch leven of Bruce. I did (and ſtill do) perceive a certain likeneſs between the two ſtories; but certainly not a ſufficient one to juſtify my

aſſertion. I feel it my Duty therefore to apologize
to the Author & the Public for this raſhneſs; and
my ſenſe of honeſty would not have been ſatisfied
by the bare omiſſion of the note. No one can ſee
ly
more clear[*neſs*] than myſelf the *littleneſs* & futility
of imagining plagiariſms in [*the*] the works of men
of Genius; but nemo omnibus horis ſapit, and my
mind, at the time of writing that note, was ſick &
ſore with anxiety, and weakened thro' much ſuffering.
I have not the moſt [*knowlege*] diſtant knowlege
of Mr Rogers, except as a correct & elegant Poet.
If any of my readers ſhould know him perſonally,
ing him
they would oblige me by inform[*er*] that I have
expiated a ſentence of unfounded detraction by a*n*
[*ſenten*] unſolicited & ſelf-originating apology.

readmitted
Having from theſe motives [*retained*] two, & thoſe
the longeſt of the poems, I had omitted, I [*gave a*]

yielded a paſſport to the three others, which [*had*] were recommended by the greateſt number of votes.—There are ſome Lines too of Lloyd's & Lambs in this appendix. They had been omitted in the former part of the volume partly by accident; but I have reaſon to believe, that the Authors regard them, as of inferior merit; & they are [*they*] are therefore rightly placed, where they will receive ſome beauty from their vicinity to others much worſe.

---

1. To Joſeph Cottle, Author of &c
2. An Effuſion on an Autumnal Evening, written in early Youth.
3. Verſes in the manner of Spencer.
4. The Compoſition of a Kiſs.

5th. To an Infant.

Then Lamb's & Lloyd's.

[MS.]

[Yet thou more bright than all the Angel Blaze
That harbinger'd thy birth, thou, Man of Woes
Despised GALILÆAN! *For the Great*
Invisible (by symbols only seen)
Seems with peculiar & unsullied light
To shine from forth th' oppressed Good Man's face,]

[MS.]

[*Religious Muſings, a deſultory Poem written on the Chriſtmas Eve of* 1794.

This is the time, when, moſt divine to hear
The voice of Adoration rouſes me,
As with a Cherub's trump: till high upborne
Yea, mingling with the Quire, I ſeem to view
The Viſion of the heavenly Multitude,
That hymn'd the ſong of Peace o'er Bethlehem's fields
[*Making the midnight glorious*
Yet more bright,]
Yet thou more bright than all the Angel Hoſt
That harbinger'd thy birth, thou, Man of Woes
Deſpiſed Galilæan! For the Great
Inviſible (*by ſymbols only ſeen*)]

[MS.]

[With a peculiar and surpassing Light 12
Shines from the visage of th' oppress'd Good Man,
When heedless of himself the scourged Saint [15]
Mourns for the' Oppressor. [Son of the most high]
[Preeminent]   Fair [is] the Vernal mead, 15
[*in*] the high
Fair [the high] Grove, the Sea, the Sun, the Stars;
o
Yet nor high Grove nor many-col[ou]r'd mead
[Bright Impress each of their creating Sire!]
Nor the green Ocean with his thousand Isles [20]
Nor the starr'd Azure, nor the sovran Sun [20]
E'er with such majesty of portraiture 20
Imag'd the unimaginable God
iour e
As thou, meek Sav[ior]! at th[at] fearful hour
When thy insulted Anguish &c.]

[When all of Self regardleſs the ſcourg'd Saint
Mourns for th' Oppreſſor. O thou meekeſt Man!
Meek Man and lowlieſt of the Sons of Men!
Who thee beheld thy imag'd Father ſaw.
His Power and Wiſdom from thy awful eye
Blended their beams, and loftier Love ſate there
Muſing on human weal, and that dread hour]
When thy inſulted Anguiſh wing'd the prayer
Harp'd by Archangels, when they ſing of Mercy!
Which when th' ALMIGHTY heard, from forth his Throne
fill'd Heaven with extacy—
Diviner light [*flaſh'd extacy o'er Heaven!*]
Heav'n's hymnings paus'd: and Hell her yawning mouth
Clos'd a brief moment.

Lovely was the Death

Of Him, whoſe Life was Love! Holy with power

He on the thought-benighted Sceptic beam'd

Manifeſt Godhead, melting into day

floating Miſts of dark

What [*Miſts dim-floating of*] Idolatry

Broke

[*Split*] and miſhap'd the Omnipreſent Sire:

[*And firſt by* TERROR, *Mercy's ſtartling prelude,*

Soul

Uncharm'd the [*Spirit*] *ſpell-bound with earthly luſts*]

Till of it's nobler Nature it 'gan feel

Dim recollections; and thence ſoar'd to HOPE,

Strong to believe whate'er of myſtic good

Not ſmall cap. Th' ETERNAL dooms for his IMMORTAL Sons.

\+ firmer +

From HOPE and [*ſtronger*] FAITH to perfect LOVE

Attracted and abſorb'd: and center'd there

GOD only to behold, and know, and feel,

Till by excluſive Conſciouſneſs of GOD

[MS.]

Note to line 34.

Τό Νοητὸν διηρήκασιν ἐις πολλῶν Θεῶν ἰδιότητας. Damas. de myſt. Ægypt.

34th [& 35th] line[s] thus

[Renewer of the ancient Truth! And firſt

By TERROR *he uncharm'd the ſlumb'ring Spirit,]*

And firſt by FEAR uncharm'd the drouſed ſoul,

Till of it's nobler &c.

[MS.]

Note to line 44.

See this *demonſtrated* by [*vide Hartley & Piſtorius*] Hartley, Vol. I. p. 114, & Vol. II^{d}. p. 329. See it likewiſe proved, and freed from the charge of myſticiſm, by Piſtorius in his Notes & Additions to part ſecond of Hartley on Man. Addition the 18th the 653rd page of the third Volume of Hartley;—octavo Edition.

All ſelf-annihilated it ſhall make
GOD it's Identity: God all in all!
We and our Father ONE!

And bleſt are they,
Who in this fleſhly World, the elect of Heaven,
Their ſtrong eye darting thro' the deeds of Men
Adore with ſtedfaſt unpreſuming gaze
Him, Nature's Eſſence, Mind, and Energy!
And gazing, trembling, patiently aſcend
Treading beneath their feet all viſible things
As ſteps, that upward to their Father's Throne
Lead gradual—elſe nor glorified nor lov'd.
THEY nor Contempt imboſom nor Revenge:
For THEY dare know of what may ſeem deform
The SUPREME FAIR ſole Operant: in whoſe ſight

All things are pure, his ſtrong controlling Love
Alike from all educing perfect good.

Their's too celeſtial courage, inly arm'd——
Dwarfing Earth's giant brood, what time they muſe
On their great Father, great beyond compare!
And marching onwards view high o'er their heads
His waving Banners of Omnipotence.

Who the Creator love, created might
Dread not: within their tents no Terrors walk.
For they are Holy Things before the Lord
Aye-unprofan'd, tho' Earth ſhould league with Hell!
God's Altar graſping with an eager hand
Fear, the wild-viſag'd, pale, eye-ſtarting wretch,
Sure-refug'd hears his hot purſuing fiends

79 [80] All things of terrible ſeeming: yea, unmov'd
Views e'en th' immitigable Miniſters
That ſhower down vengeance on theſe latter days.
For kindling with intenſer Deity
From the celeſtial MERCY-SEAT they come,
And at the revovating Wells of LOVE
Have fill'd their Vials with ſalutary Wrath

Yell at vain diſtance. Soon refreſh'd from Heaven
He calms the throb and tempeſt of his heart.
His countenance ſettles : a ſoft ſolemn bliſs
Swims in his eye : his ſwimming eye uprais'd :
And Faith's whole armour glitters on his limbs!
And thus transfigured with a dreadleſs awe,
A ſolemn huſh of ſoul, meek he beholds
All things of terrible ſeeming. [*Yea, and there,*
Unſhudder'd, unaghaſted, he ſhall view
E'en the SEVEN SPIRITS, *who in the latter day*
blaſting
Will ſhower hot [peſtilence] on the ſons of men.
For he ſhall know, his heart ſhall underſtand,
That kindling with intenſer Deity
They from the MERCY-SEAT*—like roſy flames,*
leapt forth
From God's Celeſtial MERCY-SEAT *[will flaſh],*
And at the wells of renovating LOVE

Fill their Seven Vials with ſalutary wrath,]
To ſickly Nature more medicinal
That what ſoft balm the weeping good man pours
Into the lone deſpoiled trav'ller's wounds!

Thus from th' Elect, regenerate thro' faith,
Paſs the dark Paſſions and what thirſty Cares
Drink up the ſpirit and the dim regards
Self-center. Lo they vaniſh! or acquire
New names, new features — by ſupernal grace
Enrob'd with Light, and naturaliz'd in Heaven.
As when a Shepherd on a vernal morn
Thro' ſome thick fog creeps tim'rous with ſlow foot,
Darkling he fixes on th' immediate road
His downward eye: all elſe of faireſt kind
Hid or deform'd. But lo, the burſting Sun!

[MS.]

Note to Line 90.

Our evil paſſions under the influence of Religion become innocent & may be made to animate our virtues—in the ſame manner as the thick miſt melted by the Sun increaſes the Light, which it had before excluded.

In the preceding paragraph agreeably to this Truth we had allegorically narrated the transfiguration of Fear into holy Awe.

Touch'd by th' enchantment of that ſudden beam
Strait the black vapor melteth, and in globes
Of dewy glitter gems each plant and tree :
On every leaf, on every blade it hangs !
Dance glad the new-born intermingling rays,
And wide around the landſcape ſtreams with glory !

There is one Mind, one omnipreſent Mind,
Omnific. His moſt holy name is LOVE.
Truth of ſubliming import! with the which
Who feeds and ſaturates his conſtant ſoul,
He from his ſmall particular orbit flies
With bleſt outſtarting ! From HIMSELF he flies,
Stands in the Sun, and with no partial gaze
Views all creation, and he loves it all,
And bleſſes it, and calls it very good!

This is indeed to dwell with the moſt High!
Cherubs and rapture-trembling Seraphim
Can preſs no nearer to th' Almighty's Throne.
But that we roam unconſcious, or with hearts
Unfeeling of our univerſal Sire,
And that in his vaſt family no Cain
Injures uninjur'd (in her beſt-aim'd blow
Victorious MURDER a blind Suicide)
Haply for this ſome younger Angel now
Looks down on Human Nature: and, behold!
A ſea of blood beſtrew'd with wrecks, where mad
Embattling INTERESTS on each other ruſh
With unhelm'd Rage!

'Tis the ſublime of man,
Our noontide Majeſty, to know ourſelves

[MS.]

Note to 135th Line.

If to make aught but the ſupreme Reality
the object of final purſuit — the
[*our ruling Paſſion*] be Superſtition, if [*falſely to*] attri-
but[*e*]ing of ſublime properties to things, or perſons,
which thoſe things or perſons neither do or can poſſeſs,
be ſuperſtition; then Avarice & Ambition are
Superſtitions: and he, who wiſhes to eſtimate the
evils of Superſtition, ſhould tranſport himſelf, not
to
to the temple[*s*] of [*Mex*] the Mexican Deities but ^ the
plains of Flanders, or the coaſt of Africa.—Such is
ed
the ſentiment convey[*ing*] in this & the ſubſequent
Lines.

Parts and proportions of one wond'rous whole :
This fraternizes man, this conſtitutes
Our charities and bearings. But 'tis God
Diffus'd thro' all, that doth make all one whole ;
This the worſt ſuperſtition, him except,
Aught to deſire, SUPREME REALITY !
The plenitude and permanence of bliſs !
[*O Fiends of SUPERSTITION ! not that oft*
Your pitileſs rites have floated with man's blood
The ſkull-pil'd Temple, not for this ſhall wrath
Thunder againſt you from the Holy One !
But (whether ye th' unclimbing Bigot mock
With ſecondary Gods, or if more pleas'd
Ye petrify th' [*imbrothell'd*] *Atheiſt's heart,*
The Atheiſt your worſt ſlave) I o'er ſome plain
Peopled with Death, and to the ſilent Sun

Steaming with tyrant-murder'd multitudes ;
Or where mid groans and ſhrieks loud-laughing TRADE
human
More hideous packs his bales of [living] anguiſh ;]
I will raiſe up a mourning, O ye Fiends!
And curſe your ſpells, that film the eye of Faith[;],
Hiding the preſent God[,] ; whoſe preſence loſt,
The moral world's coheſion, we become
An Anarchy of Spirits! Toy-bewitch'd,
Made blind by luſts, diſherited of ſoul,
No common center Man, no common ſire
Knoweth! A ſordid ſolitary thing,
Mid countleſs brethren with a lonely heart
Thro' courts and cities the ſmooth Savage roams
Feeling himſelf, his own low Self the whole,
When he by ſacred ſympathy might make

[MS.]

O Fiends of Superstition ! not that, oft
The erring Prieſt hath ſtain'd with Brother's blood,
Your griſly Idols, not for this may Wrath
Thunder againſt you from the Holy One !
But o'er ſome plain, that ſteameth to the Sun
Peopled with Death ; or where more hideous Trade
Loud-laughing packs his bales of human anguiſh ;

[MS.]

Note to line 160.

January 21st 1794, in the debate on the Addrefs to his Majefty, on the Speech from the Throne, the Earl of Guildford moved an amendment to the following effect: "That the Houfe hoped, His Majefty would feize the earlieft opportunity to [a] conclude a peace with France &c." [Op] This motion was oppofed by the Duke of Portland, who "confidered the war to be merely grounded on one principle—the prefervation of the CHRISTIAN RELIGION. May 30th, 1794, the Duke of Bedford moved a number of Refolutions with a view to the eftablifhment of a Peace with France. He was oppofed (among others) by Lord Abingdon in thefe remarkable words; "The beft road to Peace, my Lords! is WAR; and WAR carried on in the fame manner, in which we are taught to worfhip our CREATOR, namely, with all our fouls, and with all our minds, and with all our hearts, & with all our ftrength."

The whole ONE SELF! SELF, that no alien knows!
SELF, far diffus'd as Fancy's wing can travel!
SELF, ſpreading ſtill! Oblivious of it's own,
Yet all of all poſſeſſing! This is FAITH!
This the MESSIAH's deſtin'd victory!

But firſt offences needs muſt come! Even now
(Black Hell laughs horrible—to hear the ſcoff!)
THEE to defend, meek Galilæan! THEE
And thy mild laws of Love unutterable,
Miſtruſt and Enmity have burſt the bands
Of ſocial Peace; and liſt'ning Treachery lurks
With *pious* fraud to ſnare a brother's life;
And childleſs widows o'er the groaning land
Wail numberleſs; and orphans weep for bread!
THEE to defend, dear Saviour of Mankind!

Thee, Lamb of God! Thee, blameleſs Prince of Peace!
From all ſides ruſh the thirſty brood of war!
Austria, and that foul Woman of the North,
The luſtful Murd'reſs of her wedded Lord!
And he, connatural Mind! whom (in their ſongs
So bards of elder time had haply feign'd)
Some Fury fondled in her hate to man,
mazy ſurge
Bidding her ſerpent hair in [*tortuous folds*]
n
Lick his young face, and at his mouth i[*m*]breathe
Horrible ſympathy! And leagued with theſe
Each petty German Princeling, nurs'd in gore!
Soul-harden'd barterers of human blood!
Death's prime Slave-merchants! Scorpion-whips of Fate!
Nor leaſt in ſavagery of holy zeal,
Apt for the yoke, the race degenerate,
Whom Britain erſt had bluſh'd to call her ſons!

[MS.]

A new paragraph

Note to Line 193.

Art thou not from everlaſting, O Lord, mine Holy One? **We ſhall** not die. O Lord, thou has ordained them for Judgment, &c. Habakkuk I. 12. In this paragraph the Author recalls himſelf from his indignation againſt the inſtruments of Evil, to contemplate the *uſes* of theſe Evils in the great proceſs of divine Benevolence. In the firſt age Men were innocent from ignorance of vice; they fell, that by the knowlege of conſequences they might attain intellectual ſecurity—i.e. [*which*] Virtue, which is a wiſe & ſtrong-nerv'd Innocence.

THEE to defend the Moloch Prieſt prefers
The prayer of hate, and bellows to the herd
That Deity, ACCOMPLICE Deity
In the fierce jealouſy of waken'd wrath
Will go forth with our armies and our fleets
To ſcatter the red ruin on their foes!
O blaſphemy! to mingle fiendiſh deeds
With bleſſedneſs Lord of unſleeping Love,
From everlaſting Thou! We ſhall not die.
Theſe, even theſe, in mercy didſt thou form,
Teachers of Good thro' Evil, by brief wrong
Making Truth lovely, and her future might
Magnetic o'er the fix'd untrembling heart.

In the primeval age a dateleſs while
The vacant Shepherd wander'd with his flock

Pitching his tent where'er the green graſs wav'd.
But ſoon Imagination conjur'd up
An hoſt of new deſires : with buſy aim,
Each for himſelf, Earth's eager children toil'd.
So Property began, twy-ſtreaming fount,
Whence Vice and Virtue flow, honey and gall.
Hence the soft couch, and many-colour'd robe,
The timbrel, and arch'd dome and coſtly feaſt
With all th' inventive arts, that nurs'd the ſoul
To forms of beauty, and by ſenſual wants
Unſenſualiz'd the mind, which in the means
Learnt to forget the groſsneſs of the end,
Beſt-pleaſur'd with it's own activity.
And hence Diſeaſe that withers manhood's arm,
The dagger'd Envy, ſpirit-quenching Want,
Warriors, and Lords, and Prieſts—all the ſore ills

[MS.]

⸓ ⸓ ⸓ Such as the blind Ionian fabled erſt 224

= A new paragraph.

That vex and deſolate our mortal life :
Wide-waſting ills ! yet each th' immediate ſource
Of mightier good. Their keen neceſſities
To ceaſeleſs action goading human thought
Have made Earth's reaſoning animal her Lord ;
And the pale-featur'd Sage's trembling hand
Strong as an hoſt of armed Deities[!],
From Avarice thus, from Luxury and War
Sprang neavenly Science : and from Science Freedom.
O'er waken'd realms Philoſophers and Bards
Spread in concentric circles : they whoſe ſouls
Conſcious of their high dignities from God
Brook not Wealth's rivalry ; and they who long
Enamour'd with the charms of order hate
Th' unſeemly diſproportion ; and whoe'er
Turn with mild ſorrow from the victor's car

And the low puppetry of thrones, to muſe
On that bleſt triumph, when the PATRIOT SAGE
Call'd the red lightnings from th' o'er-ruſhing cloud
And daſh'd the beauteous Terrors on the earth
Smiling majeſtic. Such a phalanx ne'er
Meaſur'd firm paces to the calming ſound
Of Spartan flute! Theſe on the fated day,
When, ſtung to rage by Pity, eloquent men
Have rous'd with pealing voice th' unnumber'd tribes
That toil and groan and bleed, hungry and blind,
Theſe huſh'd awhile with patient eye ſerene
Shall watch the mad careering of the ſtorm;
Then o'er the wild and wavy chaos ruſh
And tame th' outrageous maſs, with plaſtic might
Moulding Confuſion to ſuch perfect forms,
As erſt were wont, bright viſions of the day!

To float before them, when, the Summer noon,
Beneath ſome arch'd romantic rock reclin'd
They felt the ſea-breeze lift their youthful locks,
Or in the month of bloſſoms, at mild eve,
Wandering with deſultory feet inhal'd
The wafted perfumes, and the flocks and woods
And many-tinted ſtreams and ſetting Sun
With all his gorgeous company of clouds
Extatic gaz'd! then homeward as they ſtray'd
Caſt the ſad eye to earth, and inly mus'd
Why there was Miſery in a world ſo fair.

Ah far remov'd from all that glads the ſenſe,
From all that ſoftens or ennobles Man,
The wretched Many! Bent beneath their loads
They gape at pageant Power, nor recognize
Their cots' tranſmuted plunder! From the tree

Of Knowledge, ere the vernal ſap had riſen,
Bleſſed
Rudely diſbranch'd! [O *bleſt*] Society!
Fitlieſt depictur'd by ſome ſun-ſcorcht waſte,
Where oft majeſtic thro' the tainted noon
The SIMOOM ſails, before whoſe purple pomp
Who falls not proſtrate dies! And where, by night,
Faſt by each precious fountain on green herbs
The lion couches; or hyæna dips
Deep in the lucid ſtream his bloody jaws;
plants
Or ſerpent [*rolls*] his vaſt moon-glittering bulk,
Caught in whoſe monſtrous twine Behemoth yells,
His bones loud craſhing!

O ye numberleſs,
Whom foul Oppreſſion's ruffian gluttony
Drives from life's plenteous feaſt! O thou poor Wretch,

267 Blessed Society !

Note.

276. Behemoth in Hebrew ſignifies wild beaſts in general. Some believe it is the elephant, ſome the Hippopotamus, ſome affirm it is the wild-bull. Poetically it deſignates any large Quadruped.

[MS.]

O loathly Suppliants! ye, that unreceiv'd
Totter heart-broken from the cloſing Gates
Of the full Lazar-houſe; or gazing, ſtand
Sick with despair! O ye to Glory's field
Forc'd or enſnar'd, who as ye gaſp in death
Bleed with new wounds beneath the Vulture's Beak!

Who nurs'd in darkneſs and made wild by want
Roameſt
[*Doſt roam*] for prey, yea thy unnatural hand
Doſt lift
[*Lifteſt*] to deeds of blood! O pale-eyed Form,
The victim of ſeduction, doom'd to know
Polluted nights and days of blaſphemy;
Who in loath'd orgies with lewd waſſailers
Muſt gaily laugh, while thy remember'd Home
Gnaws like a viper at thy ſecret heart!
O aged Women! ye who weekly catch
The morſel toſt by law-forc'd Charity,
And die ſo ſlowly, that none call it murder!
[*O loathly-viſag'd Suppliants! ye that oft*
Rack'd with diſeaſe, from the unopen'd gate
Of the full Lazar-houſe, heart-broken crawl!
O ye to ſcepter'd Glory's gore-drench'd field
Forc'd or enſnar'd, who ſwept by Slaughter's ſcythe,

(*Stern nurſe of Vultures!*) *ſteam in putrid heaps!*]
O thou poor Widow, who in dreams doſt view
Thy huſband's mangled corſe, and from ſhort doze
Start'ſt with a ſhriek: or in thy half-thatch'd cot
Wak'd by the wintry night-ſtorm, wet and cold,
Cowr'ſt
[*Cow'reſt*] o'er thy ſcreaming baby! Reſt awhile,
Children of Wretchedneſs! More groans muſt riſe,
More blood muſt ſteam, or ere your wrongs be full.
Yet is the day of Retribution nigh:
The Lamb of God hath open'd the fifth ſeal:
And upward ruſh on ſwifteſt wing of fire
Th' innumerable multitude of Wrongs
By man on man inflicted! Reſt awhile,
Children of Wretchedneſs! The hour is nigh:
And lo! the Great, the Rich, the Mighty Men,
The Kings and the Chief Captains of the World,

[MS.]

Note 316.

This paſſage alludes to the French Revolution: and the ſubſequent paragraph to the downfall of Religious Eſtabliſhments. I am convinced, that the Babylon of the Apocalypſe does not apply to Rome exclusively; but to the union of Religion with Power & Wealth, wherever it is found.

With all that fix'd on high like ſtars of Heaven
Shot baleful influence, ſhall be caſt to earth,
Vile and down-trodden, as the untimely fruit
Shook from the fig-tree by a ſudden ſtorm.
Ev'n now the ſtorm begins: each gentle name,
Faith and meek Piety, with fearful joy
Tremble far-off — for lo! the Giant FRENZY
Uprooting empires with his whirlwind arm
Mocketh high Heaven; burſt hideous from the cell
Where the old Hag, unconquerable, huge,
Creation's eyeless drudge, black RUIN, ſits
Nurſing th' impatient earthquake.
O return!
Pure FAITH! meek PIETY! The abhorred Form
Whoſe ſcarlet robe was ſtiff with earthly pomp,
Who drank iniquity in cups of gold,

Whoſe names were many and all blaſphemous,
Hath met the horrible judgement! Whence that cry?
The mighty army of foul Spirits ſhriek'd,
Diſherited of earth! For She hath fallen
On whoſe black front was written MYSTERY;
She that reel'd heavily, whoſe wine was blood;
She that work'd whoredom with the DÆMON POWER
And from the dark embrace all evil things
Brought forth and nurtur'd: mitred ATHEISM
And patient FOLLY who on bended knee
Gives back the ſteel that ſtabb'd him; and pale FEAR
ſhapings
Hunted by ghaſtlier [*terrors*] than ſurround
Moon-blaſted Madneſs when he yells at midnight!
Return pure FAITH! return meek PIETY!
The kingdoms of the world are your's: each heart
Self-govern'd, the vaſt family of Love
Rais'd from the common earth by common toil

[MS.]

in hour of
When [*on*] ſome [*high and*] ſolemn jubilee
maſſy
The [*mighty*] Gates of Paradiſe are thrown
Wide open, and forth come in fragments wild
Sweet echoes of unearthly melodies,
And Odors ſnatch'd from beds of Amaranth,

Enjoy the equal produce. Such delights
As float to earth, permitted viſitants!
[When on ſome ſolemn jubilee of Saints [*ſaintly*] *
The ſapphire-blazing gates of Paradiſe
Are thrown wide open, and thence voyage forth
Detachments wild of ſeraph-warbled airs,
And odors ſnatch'd from beds of amaranth,]
And they, that from the chryſtal river of life
Spring up on freſhen'd wing, ambroſial gales!
The favor'd good man in his lonely walk
Perceives them, and his ſilent ſpirit drinks
Strange bliſs which he ſhall recognize in heaven.
And ſuch delights, ſuch ſtrange beatitude
Seize on my young anticipating heart
When that bleſt future ruſhes on my view!

* [*Saintly*] is in Cottle's hand.—*Ed.*

For in his own and in his Father's might
the THOUSAND YEARS
The SAVIOUR comes! While as [*to ſolemn ſtrains*]
Lead up their myſtic dance, the DESERT ſhouts!
[*The THOUSAND YEARS lead up their myſtic dance,*]
Old OCEAN claps his hands! [*the DESERT ſhouts!*
[*breezes of an equal Spring*]
[*And ſoft gales wafted from the haunts of Spring*
Melt the primæval North!] The mighty Dead
Riſe to new life, whoe'er from earlieſt time
With conſcious zeal had urg'd Love's wond'rous plan,
Coadjutors of God. To MILTON's trump
The high Groves of the renovated earth
[*The odorous groves of earth reparadis'd*]
Unboſom their glad echoes: inly huſh'd
Adoring NEWTON his ſerener eye
Raiſes to heaven: and he of mortal kind
Wiſeſt, he* firſt who mark'd the ideal tribes
Up thro'
[*Down*] the fine fibres [*from*] the ſentient brain

* David Hartley.

[MS.]

360. The Millennium: in which I ſuppoſe that man will continue to enjoy the higheſt glory, of which his human nature is capable. That all who in paſt ages have endeavoured to ameliorate the ſtate of man, will riſe & enjoy the fruits & flowers, the imperceptible ſeeds of which they had ſown in their former Life: and that the wicked will during the ſame period be ſuffering the remedies adapted to their ſeveral bad habits. [*that*] I ſuppoſe that this period will be followed by the paſſing away of this Earth, & by our entering [*on*] the ſtate of pure intellect; when all creation ſhall reſt from its labors.

[MS.]

[Ye ſweep before me in as lovely Hues
As ſtream, reflected, from the veiling plumes
Of them, that aye before the Jaſper Throne
Adoring bend. Bleſt Years! ye too depart,]

Note to Line 385.

[*The*] Revel. Ch. IV. v. 2 & 3rd.—And immediately I was in the Spirit; and behold a Throne was ſet in Heaven, and one ſat on the throne. And he that ſat was to look like a jaſper & ſardine ſtone, &c.

[Roll ſubtly-ſurging. Preſſing on his ſteps
Lo! Prieſtley there, Patriot, and Saint, and Sage, Small cap.
Whom that my fleſhly eye hath never ſeen
A childiſh pang of impotent regret
Hath thrill'd my heart. Him from his native land
Stateſmen blood-ſtain'd and Prieſts idolatrous
[*By dark lies mad'ning the blind multitude*]
Drove with vain hate: calm, pitying he retir'd,
And mus'd expectant on theſe promis'd years.

O Years! the bleſt preeminence of Saints!
[*Sweeping before the rapt prophetic Gaze*
Bright as what glories of the jaſper throne
Stream from the gorgeous and face-veiling plumes
Of Spirits adoring! Ye, bleſt Years! muſt end,]]
And all beyond is darkneſs! Heights moſt ſtrange[!],

Whence Fancy falls, fluttering her idle wing.

For who of woman born may paint the hour,

When seiz'd in his mid courſe the Sun ſhall wane

Making noon ghaſtly! Who of woman born

thought
the workings of his [*ſpirit*]
May image in [*his wildly-working thought,*]

[MS.]

Note to 391. The final Deſtruction imperſonated.

How the black-viſag'd, red-eyed Fiend outſtretcht

Beneath th' unſteady feet of Nature groans,

In feveriſh ſlumbers — deſtin'd then to wake,

When fiery whirlwinds thunder his dread name

And Angels ſhout, DESTRUCTION! How his arm

laſt great
The [*mighty*] Spirit lifting high in air

Shall ſwear by him, the ever-living ONE,

TIME IS NO MORE!

Believe thou, O my ſoul,

Life is a viſion ſhadowy of Truth,

398
[MS.] Note to line [400]. This paragraph is intelligible [*who*] to those who, like the Author, believe & feel the ſublime ſyſtem of Berkley; & the doctrine of the final Happineſs of all men.

And vice, and anguiſh, and the wormy grave,
Shapes of a dream! The veiling clouds retire,
And lo! the Throne of the redeeming God
Forth flaſhing unimaginable day
Wraps in one blaze earth, heaven, and deepeſt hell.

Contemplant Spirits! ye that hover o'er
With untir'd gaze th' immeaſurable fount
Ebullient with creative Deity!
And ye of plaſtic power, that interfus'd
Roll thro' the groſſer and material maſs
In organizing ſurge! Holies of God!
(And what if Monads of the infinite mind?)
I haply journeying my immortal courſe
Shall ſometime join your myſtic choir! Till then
I diſcipline my young noviciate thought

In miniſteries of heart-ſtirring ſong,
And aye on Meditation's heaven-ward wing
Soaring aloft I breathe th' empyreal air
Of Love, omnific, omnipreſent Love,
Whoſe day-ſpring riſes glorious in my ſoul
As the great Sun, when he his influence
Sheds on the froſt-bound waters—The glad ſtream
Flows to the ray and warbles as it flows.

[*N O T E S*

ON

RELIGIOUS MUSINGS.

LINE 8.

And ſuddenly there was with the Angel a multitude of the heavenly Hoſt, praiſing God and ſaying glory to God in the higheſt and on earth peace.

LUKE II. 13.]

12th
LINE [27.]

Philip ſaith unto him, Lord! ſhew us the Father and it ſufficeth us. Jeſus ſaith unto him, Have I been ſo long time with you, and yet haſt thou not known me, Philip? He that hath ſeen me hath ſeen the Father.

JOHN XIV. 9.

85.
LINE [91]

And I heard a great voice out of the Temple ſaying to the ſeven Angels, pour out the vials of the wrath of God upon the earth.

REVELATION XVI. 1.

LINE [193] 174.

That Deſpot, who received the wages of an hireling that he might act the part of a ſwindler, and who ſkulked from his impotent attacks on the liberties of France to perpetrate more ſucceſsful iniquity in the plains of *Poland.*

LINE [200] 181.

The Father of the preſent Prince of Heſſe Caſſell ſupported himſelf and his ſtrumpets at Paris by the vaſt ſums which he received from the Britiſh Government during the American war for the fleſh of his ſubjects.

LINE [212] 193.

Art thou not from everlafting, O Lord, mine Holy One? We fhall not die. O Lord! thou haft ordained them for judgment, &c.

HABAKKUK I. 12.

[*LINE* 235.

I deem that the teaching of the gofpel for hire is wrong; becaufe it gives the teacher an improper bias in favor of particular opinions on a fubject where it is of the laft importance that the mind fhould be perfectly unbiaffed. Such is my private opinion; but I mean not to cenfure all hired teachers, many among whom I know, and venerate as the beft and wifeft of men—God forbid that I fhould think of thefe, when I ufe the word PRIEST, *a name, after which any other term of abhorrence would appear an anti-climax. By a* PRIEST *I mean a man who holding the ſcourge of power in his right hand and a bible (tranſlated by authority) in his left, doth neceſſarily cauſe the bible and the ſcourge to be aſſociated ideas, and ſo produces that temper of mind that leads to Infidelity — Infidelity which judging of Revelation by the doctrines and practices of eſtabliſhed Churches honors God by rejecting Chriſt. See " Addreſs to the People," Page* 57, *ſold by Parſons, Paternoſter-Row.*]

LINE [253] 235.

DR. FRANKLIN.

LINE [288] 270.

At eleven o'clock, while we contemplated with great pleaſure the rugged top of Chiggre, to which we were faſt approaching, and where we were to ſolace ourſelves with plenty of good water, IDRIS cried out with a loud voice, 'Fall upon your faces, 'for here is the Simoom.' I ſaw from the S. E. an haze come on, in colour like the purple part of the rainbow, but not ſo compreſſed or thick.— It did not occupy twenty yards in breadth, and was about twelve feet high from the ground.—— We all lay flat on the ground, as if dead, till IDRIS told us it was blown over. The meteor, or purple haze, which I ſaw, was indeed paſſed; but the light air that ſtill blew was of heat to threaten ſuffocation.

[MS.] Add × add BRUCE'S Travels, vol. 4. page 557.

[*LINE* 294.

Uſed poetically for a very large quadruped; but in general it deſignates the Elephant.]

[MS.] × The Simoom is here introduced as emblematical of the pomp & powers of Deſpotiſm.

LINE [324] 305.

See the ſixth chapter of the Revelation of St. John the Divine. —— And I looked and beheld a pale horſe; and his name that ſat on him was Death, and Hell followed with him. And power was given unto them over the FOURTH part of the Earth to kill with ſword, and with hunger, and with peſtilence, and with the beaſts of the earth. —— And when he had opened the fifth ſeal, I ſaw under the altar the ſouls of them that were ſlain for the word of God, and for the teſtimony which they held: and white robes were given unto every one of them; and it was ſaid unto them, that they ſhould reſt yet for a little ſeaſon, until their fellow ſervants alſo, and their brethren, that ſhould be killed as they were ſhould be fulfilled. And I beheld when he had opened the ſixth ſeal, the ſtars of Heaven fell unto the Earth, even as a fig tree caſteth her untimely figs when ſhe is ſhaken of a mighty wind: And the Kings of the earth, and the great men, and the rich men, and the chief captains, &c.

[*LINE* 335.

The French Revolution.]

LINE [343] 325.

And there came one of the ſeven Angels which had the ſeven vials and talked with me, ſaying unto me, come hither! I will ſhew unto thee the judgment of the great Whore, that ſitteth upon many waters: with whom the Kings of the earth have committed fornication, &c. Revelation of St. John the Divine, chapter the ſeventeenth. [MS.] This (the 17th)

& the thirteenth Scaliger

deem'd the only intelligible chapters

of the the whole Apocalypſe.

Scaligerianis II. pag. 14 & 15.

NOTES
[ON THE
MONODY TO CHATTERTON]

POOR CHATTERTON! HERBERT CROFT has written with feeling concerning him; and VICESIMUS KNOX has ATTEMPTED to write with feeling. —— HAYLEY [*who* (*ſo future Antiquarians will inform our poſterity*) *has written ſundry things in the reign of King George the Third,*] deſcribes [*the death of*] Chatterton in his Eſſay on Poetry—as *tearing the ſtrings of his lyre in the agonies of death!!*——By far the beſt poem on this ſubject is "Neglected Genius or Tribuatry "Stanzas to the memory of the unfortunate Chat-"terton," written by RUSHTON, a blind Sailor.

WALPOLE writes thus. All the houſe of Forgery are relations. Although it be but juſt to CHATTER-

TON's Memory to ſay, that his poverty never made him claim kindred with the more enriching branches yet he who could ſo ingeniouſly counterfeit ſtyles and (the aſſerter believes) hands, might eaſily have been led to the more facile imitation of proſe promiſſary notes!"——[*O ye who honor the name of MAN, rejoice that this Walpole is called a* LORD*!*]

MILLES

[*MILES*] too, the Editor of his Poems—a Prieſt who though only a DEAN, in dullneſs and malignity was moſt *epiſcopally* eminent, foul[*y*] calumniated him——An Owl mangling a poor dead Nightingale!——

ly

[*Moſt inſpired Bard!*
To him alone in this benighted age
Was that divine Inſpiration given,
Which glows in MILTON's and in SHAKESPEARE's page,
The pomp and prodigality of Heaven.]

[MS.] Begin the page here — it is abfolutely cheatry to give fuch open print.

NOTES.

Note 1 —— Page 37.

Lee Boo, the fon of Abba Thule, Prince of the Pelew Iflands came over to England with Captain Wilfon, died of the fmall-pox, and is buried in Grenwich Church-yard. See Keate's Account.

Note 2. —— Page 37.

And fuffering Nature weeps that *one* fhould die.

Southey's Retrofpect.

Page 46.

Yet never Burke ! *thou drank'ft Corruption's bowl!*

When I compofed this line, I had not read the following paragraph in the Cambridge Intelligencer (of Saturday, November 21, 1795.)

"*When Mr. Burke firft croffed over the House of Commons from the Oppofition to the Miniftry, he*

N 2

received a pension of 1200*l. a-year charged on the King's Privy Purse!* When he had completed his labors, it was then a queſtion what recompence his ſervice deſerved. Mr. Burke wanting a preſent ſupply of money, it was thought that a penſion of 2000l. per annum *for forty years certain,* would ſell for eighteen years purchaſe, and bring him of courſe 36,000l. But this penſion muſt, by the very unfortunate act, of which Mr. Burke was himſelf the author, have come before Parliament. Inſtead of this Mr. Pitt ſuggeſted the idea of a penſion of 2000l a-year *for three lives,* to be charged on the King's Revenue of the Weſt India $4\frac{1}{8}$ per cents. This was tried at the market, but it was found that it would not produce the 36,000l. which were wanted. In conſequence of this a penſion of 2500l.

per annum, *for three lives* on the 4½ Weſt India Fund, the lives to be nominated by Mr. Burke, that he may accommodate the purchaſers, is *finally* granted to this diſintereſted patriot! He has thus retir'd from the trade of politics, with penſions to the amount of 3700l. a-year."

[*We feel not for the Public in the preſent inſtance*: *we feel for the honor of genius; and mourn to find one of her moſt richly gifted children aſſociated with the Youngs, Wynhams, and Reeveſes of the day;* "*match'd in mouth*" *with*

> "*Maſtiff, bloodhound, mungril grim*
> *Cur and ſpaniel, brache and lym*
> *Bobtail tike and trundle-tail;*"

And the reſt of that motley pack, that open in moſt hideous concert, whenever ou[*t*] *State-Nimrod pro-*

vokes the ſcent by a trail of rancid plots and falſe inſurrections! For of the rationality *of theſe animals I am inclined to entertain a doubt, a* charitable *doubt! ſince ſuch is the ſyſtem which they ſupport that we add to their integrity whatever we detract from their underſtanding:*

—— Fibris increvit opimum

Pingue: carent culpa.

It is conſoling to the lovers of human nature to reflect that Edmund Burke the only writer of that faction "whoſe name would not ſully the page of an opponent" learnt the diſcipline of genius in a different corps. At the flames which riſe from the altar of Freedom, he kindled that torch with which he ſince endeavored to ſet fire to her temple. Peace be to his ſpirit, when it departs from us: this is the ſevereſt puniſhment I wiſh him — that he may be appointed under-porter to St. Peter, and be obliged to open the gates of Heaven to Briſſot, Roland, Condorcet, Fayette, and Prieſtley!——See Number I. of the WATCHMAN, *a miſcellany publiſhed every eighth day by the Author of theſe Poems, and by Parſons, Paternoſter Row, London.*]

Note 3. —— Page 50.

Hymettian Flowrets. Hymettus a mountain near Athens, celebrated for its honey. This alludes to Mr. Sheridan's claſſical attainments, and the following four lines to the exquiſite ſweetneſs and almoſt *Italian* delicacy of his poetry.——In Shakeſpeare's "Lover's Complaint" there is a fine ſtanza almoſt prophetically charaċteriſtic of Mr. Sheridan.

So on the tip of his ſubduing tongue
All kind of argument and queſtion deep,
All replication prompt and reaſon ſtrong

For his advantage ſtill did wake and ſleep,
To make the weeper laugh, the laugher weep:
He had the dialect and different ſkill,
Catching all paſſions in his craft of will:
That he did in the general boſom reign
Of young and old.

Note 4. —— Page 52.

When *Kosciusko* was obſerved to fall, the Poliſh ranks ſet up a ſhriek.

Note 5.——Page 62.

This little Poem was written when the Author was a boy.

Note 6.——Page 65.

One night in Winter, on leaving a College-friend's room, with whom I had ſupped, I careleſly took away with me "The Robbers" a drama, the very name of which I had never before heard of:—

A Winter midnight—the wind high—and "The Robbers" for the firſt time!——The readers of SCHILLER will conceive what I felt. SCHILLER introduces no ſupernatural beings; yet his human beings agitate and aſtoniſh more than all the *goblin* rout—even of Shakeſpeare.

Note 7. —— Page

"Effinxit quondam blandum meditata laborem
Baſia laſcivâ Cypria Diva manâ.
Ambroſiæ ſuccos occultâ temperat arte,
Fragranſque infuſo nectare tin[*q*]it opus. *g*
Sufficit et partem mellis, quod ſubdolus olim
Non impune favis ſurripuiſſet [*a*]mor. *A*
Decuſſos violæ foliis admiſcet odores
Et ſpolia æſtivis [*pulrima*] rapta roſis, *plurima*
[*Adiddit*] illecebra et mille et mille lepores, *Addit et*
Et quot Acidalius guadia Ceſtus habet *s* "

[MS.] [*From the Carmina Quadrageſimalia—Vol II. To the copy in the Briſtol Library there is a manuſcript ſignature of L. Thomas to this beautiful compoſition.*]

Ex his compoſuit Dea baſia ; et omnia libans

Invenias nitidæ ſparſa per ora Cloës.

Note 8.——Page 84.

The flower hangs its head waving at times to the gale. Why doſt thou awake me, O G[*l*]ale! it ſeems to ſay, I am covered with the drops of Heaven. The time of my fading is near, the blaſt that ſhall ſcatter my leaves. To-morrow ſhall the traveller come, he that ſaw me in my beauty ſhall come. His eyes will ſearch the field, they will not find me. So ſhall they ſearch in vain for the voice of Cona, after it has failed in the field.——— BERRATHON, bid. Oſſian's Poems, vol. 2.

Note 9.—— Page 86.

How long will ye roll around me, blue-tumbling waters of ocean? My dwelling was not always in caves, nor beneath the whiſtling tree. My feaſt was ſpread in Torthoma's Hall. The youths beheld me in my lovelineſs. They bleſſed the dark-haired Nina-thomà. ——— BERRATHON.

Note 10. —— Page 99.

[MS.] Mr. Cottle will carefully compare this with the copy.

L'athee n'eſt point a mes yeux un faux eſprit ; je puis vivre avec lui auſſi bien et mieux qu'avec le devot, car il raiſonne davantage, mais il lut manque un ſens, et mon ame ne ſe fond point entièrement avec la ſienne: il eſt froid au ſpectacle le plus raviſſant, et il chercle un ſyllogiſme lorſque je rends une actione de grace,

"Appel a l'impartiale poſterite', par la Citoyenne Roland," troiſieme partie, p. 113.

Page 105.

O (have I ſigh'd) were mine the Wizard's rod!

I entreat the Public's pardon for having careleſly ſuffered to be printed ſuch intolerable ſtuff as this

and the thirteen following lines. They have not the merit even of originality; as every thought is to be found in the Greek Epigrams. The lines in this poem from the 27th to the 36th, I have been told are a palpable imitation of the paſſage from the 355th to the 370th line of the Pleaſures of Memory part 3. I do not perceive ſo ſtriking a ſimilarity between the two paſſages; [*but if it exiſt,*] at all events I had written the Effuſion ſeveral years before I had ſeen Mr. Rogers' Poem.——It may be proper to remark that the tale of Florio in "the Pleaſures of Memory" is to be found in Lochleve[*r*]; a Poem of great merit, n
by Michael Bruce.——In Mr. Rogers' Poem the names are Floria and Julia; in the Lochl[*era*] ven
Lomond and Levina—and this is all the difference. We ſeize the opportunity of deſcribing from the Lochleve[*r*] of Bruce the following exquiſite paſſage, n

deſcribing the effects of a fine day on the human heart.

Fat on the plain and mountain's ſunny ſide
Large droves of oxen and the fleecy flocks
Feed undiſturbed, and fill the echoing air.
With Muſic grateful to their Maſter's ear.
The Traveller ſtops and gazes round and round
O'er all the plains that animate his heart
With Mirth and Muſic. Even the mendicant
Bow-bent with age, that on the old gray ſtone
Sole-ſitting ſuns him in the public way,
Feels his heart leap, and to himſelf he ſings.

Note 11.——Page 111.

The expreſſion "green radiance" is borrowed from Mr. Wordsworth, a Poet whoſe verſification is occaſionally harſh and his diction too frequently obſcure: but whom I deem unrivalled among the writers of the prefent day in manly fentiment, novel imagery, and vivid colouring. [MS.] [*There is a great deal omitted here I insist on its insertion*]

Note 13. —— Page 118.

LIGHT *from plants.* In Sweden a very curious phenomenon has been obferved on certain flowers by M. Haggern, lecturer in natural history. One evening he [*pre*]ceived a faint flafh of light repeatedly dart from a marigold. Surprifed at fuch an uncommon appearance, he refolved to examine it with attention; and, to be affured it was no deception of the eye, he placed a man near him, with orders to make a fignal at the moment when he obferved the light. They both faw it conftantly at the fame moment.

The light was moft brilliant on marigolds of an orange or flame colour; but fcarcely vifible on pale ones.

The flash was frequently seen on the same flower two or three times in quick succession; but more commonly at intervals of several minutes: and when several flowers in the same place emitted their light together, it could be observed at a considerable distance.

[MS.] Good heavens! what a Gap!

This phenomenon was remarked in the months of July and August at sun-set, and for half an hour, when the atmosphere was clear; but after a rainy day, or when the air was loaded with vapours nothing of it was seen.

[MS.] Good heavens! what a Gap!

The following flowers emitted flashes, more or less vivid, in this order:

[MS.] Good Heavens! what a Gap!

1. The Marigold, *galendula officinalis.*

2. Monk's-hood, *tropælum majus.*

3. The orange-lily, *lilium bulbiferum.*

4. The Indian pink, *tagetes patula & erecta.*

From the rapidity of the flash, and other circumstances, it may be conjectured that there is something of electricity in this phenomenon.

ERRATA.

[MS.] Most inelegant

Page 22. *For froths read* froth, *and omit the comma at waves.—Page* 24. *For obedience read* obeisance. —*Page* 74. *For Like snowdrop opening to the solar ray read* As night-clos'd Flowret to the orient ray. —*Page* 124. *For An antic huge read* antic small.— *Page* 126. *Divide the third from the second Stanza.* —*Page* 127. *For the semicolon after at you will; put a comma.—Page* 128. *For Frst read* First.— *Ditto, For tempest honor'd read* tempest-honor'd.

F I N I S

[MS.] From Monk's-hood to phænomenon may very well be printed in the 191nd Page—and then let the Errata [*be*] occupy the last.

Ode

on the

Departing Year.

A

[MS.]

The Motto —! where is the
Motto — ? I would not have
lost the MOTTO for a kingdom
twas the best part of the
Ode

ARGUMENT.

The Ode commences with an Address to [the] *Divine Providence,* / [that] *regulates into one* ^ *vast Harmony all the events of time, however calamitous some of them may appear to mortals. The second Strophe calls on men to suspend their private joys and sorrows, and devote them for awhile to the cause of human nature in general. The first Epode speaks of the Empress of Russia, who died of an Apoplexy on the 17th of November 1796; having just concluded a subsidiary treaty with the Kings combined against France. The first and second Antistrophe describe the Image of the departing year, &c. as in a vision. The second Epode prophecies in anguish of spirit, the downfall of this Country.* ^

^ [*to*] ^ that
/ which
^ ,

ODE

on the

DEPARTING YEAR

[MS.] (Composed Decembr 23rd, 1796)

STROPHE I.

SPIRIT! who sweepest the wild Harp of Time,
It is most hard with an untroubled Ear
Thy dark inwoven Harmonies to hear!
Yet, mine eye fixt on Heaven's unchang[*ed*] (ing) clime,
Long had I listened free from mortal fear,
With inward stillness, and a bowed mind:
When lo! far onwards waving [*in*] (on) the wind
I saw the skirts of the DEPARTING YEAR!
    Starting from my silent sadness,
    Then with no unholy madness,
  Ere yet the entered cloud forbade my sight,
I rais'd th' impetuous song, and solemnized his flight.

6

STROPHE II.

Hither from the recent Tomb ;
From the [*p*]rison's direr gloom ;
From Poverty's heart-wasting languish ;
From Distemper's midnight anguish :
Or where his two bright torches blending
Love illumine[*'s*] Manhood's maze ;
Or where o'er cradled infants bending
Hope has fix'd her wishful gaze :
Hither, in perplexed dance,
Ye WOES, and young-eyed JOYS, advance !
By Time's wild harp, and by the Hand
Whose indefatigable Sweep
Forbids its fateful strings to sleep,
I bid you haste, a mixt tumultuous band !
From every private bower,
And each domestic hearth,
Haste for one solemn hour ;

illumine's! that villainous apostrophe * belongs to the *Genitive case of Substantives* only— it should be illumines. O that Printers were wise! O that they would read Bishop Lowth!——

And with a loud and yet a louder voice
O er Nature struggling in portentous birth
Weep and rejoice!

[*O'er Nature struggling with portentous birth!*]
Name,
Still echoes the dread [*name*] that o'er the earth

Let slip the storm and woke the brood of Hell:

And now advance in saintly Jubilee[,] /8,

JUSTICE & TRUTH[:] T[*t*]hey too have heard the spell, ^ .
^
They too obey thy name, divinest LIBERTY!

EPODE.

I mark'd Ambition in his war-array;

I heard the mailed Monarch's troublous cry —

"Ah! whither does the Northern Conqueress stay?

"Groans not her Chariot o'er its onward way?"

Fly, mailed Monarch, fly!

Stunn'd by Death's "twice mortal" mace,

No more on MURDER's lurid face

Th' insatiate Hag shall glote with drunken eye!

Manes of th' unnumbered Slain !

Ye that gasp'd on WARSAW's plain !

Ye that erst at ISMAIL's tower,

When human ruin chok'd the streams,

Fell in Conquest's glutted hour

Mid Women's shrieks and Infant's screams ;

Whose shrieks, whose screams were vain to stir

Loud-laughing, red-eyed Massacre !

Spirits of th' uncoffin'd Slain,

Sudden blasts of Triumph swelling

Oft at night, in misty train

Rush around her narrow Dwelling !

Th' exterminating Fiend is fled—

(Foul her Life and dark her Doom !)

Mighty Army of the Dead,

Dance, like Death-fires, round her Tomb !

Then with prophetic song relate

Each some sceptered Murderer's fate !

9

When shall sceptered SLAUGHTER cease?
Awhile he crouch'd O Victor France!
Beneath the lightning of thy Lance,
With treacherous dalliance wooing PEACE.
But soon up-springing from his dastard trance
The boastful, bloody son of Pride betrayed
His hatred of the blest and blessing Maid.
One cloud, O Freedom! cross'd thy orb of Light
And sure, he deem'd, that Orb was quench'd in
night:
For still does MADNESS roam on GUILT'S bleak dizzy
height!

ANTISTROPHE I.

DEPARTING YEAR! 'twas on no earthly shore
My soul beheld thy Vision. Where, alone,

"*With treacherous dalliance wooing peace.*"—At the time this Ode was being composed, our Ambassador had returned from Paris; the French Directory professing to consider his ultimatum as an insult to the Republic.

Voiceless and stern, before the Cloudy Throne
Aye Memory sits ; there, garmented with gore,
With many an unimaginable groan
Thou storiedst thy sad Hours ! Silence ensued :
Deep Silence o'er th' etherial Multitude,
Whose wreathed Locks with snow-white Glories shone.
Then, his eye wild ardors glancing,
From the choired Gods advancing,
The SPIRIT of the EARTH made reverence meet,
And stood up beautiful before the Cloudy Seat!

ANTISTROPHE II.

On every Harp, on every Tongue,
While the mute Enchantment hung [:] / ,
Like Midnight from a thunder cloud
Spake the sudden SPIRIT loud—
" Thou in stormy Blackness throning
" Love and uncreated Light,

II

" By the Earth's unsolaced groaning
" Seize thy terrors, Arm of Might!
" By Belgium's corse impeded flood!
" By Vendee steaming Brother's blood!
" By PEACE with proffer'd insult scar'd,
" Masked hate and envying scorn!
" By Years of Havoc yet unborn;
" And Hunger's bosom to the frost-winds bar'd!
" But chief by Afric's wrongs
" Strange, horrible, and foul!
" By what deep Guilt belongs
" To the deaf Senate, " full of gifts & lies!"
" By Wealth's insensate laugh! By Torture's howl!
" Avenger, rise!
" For ever shall the bloody Island scowl?

" *By Belgium's corse impeded flood!*"—The Rhine.

" For aye, unbroken, shall her cruel Bow
" Shoot Famine's arrows o'er thy ravaged World?
" Hark! how wide NATURE joins her groans below—
" Rise, God of Nature, rise! Ah why those Bolts unhurl'd?

EPODE II.

The voice had ceas'd, the Phantoms fled,
Yet still I gasp'd and reel'd with dread[.] / :
And ever when the dream of night
Renews the vision to my sight,
Cold sweat-damps gather on my limbs;
My Ears throb hot; my eyeballs start;
My Brain with horrid tumult swims;
Wild is the tempest of my Heart;
And my thick and struggling breath
Imitates the toil of Death!
No stranger agony confounds
The Soldier on the war-field spread,

When all foredone with toil & wounds[,]

Death-like he dozes among heaps of Dead!

(The strife is o'er, the day-light fled,

And the Night-wind clamours hoarse;

See the startful Wretch's head

Lies pillow'd on a Brother's Corse!)

A new paragraph ʌ ʌ ʌ —

O doom'd to fall, enslav'd and vile,

— ʌ ʌ ʌ ʌ — a new paragraph

[ʌ ʌ ʌ ʌ]

O ALBION! O my mother Isle!

Thy valleys, fair as Eden's bowers,

Glitter green with sunny showers;

Thy grassy Uplands' gentle swells

Echo to the Bleat of Flocks;

(Those grassy Hills, those glitt'ring Dells

Proudly ramparted with rocks)

And Ocean mid his uproar wild

Speaks safety to his Island-child.

Hence for many a fearless age

Has social Quiet lov'd thy shore;

Nor ever sworded Foeman's rage
Or sack'd thy towers, or stain'd thy fields with gore.
Disclaim'd of Heaven! mad Av'rice at thy side
At coward distance, yet with kindling pride[—] / ,
Safe 'mid thy herds and corn-fields thou hast stood,
And join'd the yell of Famine and of Blood.
All nations curse thee ; and with eager wond'ring
Shall hear DESTRUCTION, like a vulture, scream !
Strange-eyed DESTRUCTION, who with many a dream
Of central fires [*flames*] thro' nether seas upthund'ring
Soothes her fierce solitude ; yet as she lies

" *Disclaim'd of Heaven!* " We have been preserved by our insular situation from suffering the actual horrors of War ourselves; and we have shewn our gratitude to Providence for this immunity, by our eagerness to spread those horrors over other nations less happily [*situated*] circumstance

Of the one hundred and seven last years fifty have been years of War.

By livid fount or roar of blazing stream,

[*In the black chamber of a sulphur'd mount,*] δ

If ever to her lidless dragon eyes,

O Albion! thy predestin'd ruins rise,

The Fiend-hag on her perilous couch doth leap,

Mutt'ring distemper'd triumph in her charmed sleep.

Away, my soul, away!

In vain, in vain, the birds of warning sing—

And hark! I hear the famin'd brood of prey

lank

Flap their [*dark*] pennons on the groaning wind! lank

Away, my soul, away!

I unpartaking of the evil thing,

With daily prayer[,] and daily toil[,] δ, δ,

Soliciting for food my scanty soil,

Have wail'd my country with a loud lament.

Now I recenter my immortal mind

[MS.] I suspect, almost suspect, that the word "dark" was *intentionally* substituted for "lank"—if so, 'twas the most *tasteless* thing thou ever didst, dear Joseph!—

16

In the long sabbath of high self-content;
Cleans'd from the fears and anguish that bedim
God's image, Sister of the Seraphim.

[MS.] Decemb. 23rd
1796

[MS.]

The Melancholy Man

The Maniac

The infant

To the Genius of Shakespere

Stanzas after a Journey into N. Wales.

—

The Sonnets

=

Lines to S. T. Coleridge

Christmas, a Poem

—

Poems on the Death
Priscilla Farmer

Ode

on the

Departing Year.

[MS.]

Motto

I beseech you, let the Motto be printed; and printed accurately.

O D E

on the

DEPARTING YEAR.

STROPHE I.

SPIRIT ! who sweepest the wild Harp of Time,
It is most hard with an untroubled Ear
Thy dark inwoven Harmonies to hear !
Yet, mine eye fixt on Heaven's unchang[*ed*] clime, / ing
Long had I listened, free from mortal fear,
With inward stillness, and a bowed mind :
When lo ! far onward waving [*in*] the wind on
I saw the skirts of the DEPARTING YEAR !
Starting from my silent sadness
Then with no unhŏly·madness,
Ere yet the entered cloud forbade my sight,
I rais'd th' impetuous song, and solemnized his flight.

[MS.] "Ode on the departing Year." This Ode was written on the 24th 25th and 26th days of December, 1796 ; and published separately on the last day of the year.

6

STROPHE II.

Hither from the recent tomb ;
From the prison's direr gloom ;
From Poverty's heart-wasting languish ;
From Distemper's midnight anguish :
Or where his two bright torches blending
Love illumine[']s Manhood's maze ;
Or where o'er cradled infants bending
Hope has fix'd her wishful gaze :
Hither, in perplexed dance,
Ye Woes, and young-eyed Joys, advance!
By Time's wild harp, and by the Hand
Whose indefatigable Sweep
Forbids its fateful strings to sleep,
I bid you haste, a mixt tumultuous band!
From every private bower,
And each domestic hearth,
Haste for one solemn hour ;

7

And with a loud & yet a louder voice

[*MS. in Cottle's hand. Ed.*] O'er Nature struggling [*with*] in portentous birth

Weep and rejoice!

[*O'er Nature struggling with portentous birth!*]

Still echoes the dread [*n*]ame that o'er the earth N

Let slip the storm and woke the brood of Hell:

And now advance in saintly Jubilee[,] δ

JUSTICE and TRUTH: they too have heard the spell,

They too obey thy [*n*]ame, divinest LIBERTY! N

EPODE.

I mark'd Ambition in his war-array;

I heard the mailed Monarch's troublous cry—

"Ah! [*whither*] wherefore does the Northern Conqueress stay?

"Groans not her Chariot o'er its onward way?"

Fly, mailed Monarch, fly!

Stunn'd by Death's "twice mortal" mace,

No more on MURDER's lurid face

Th' insatiate Hag shall glote with drunken eye!

[MS.] O'er Nature ſtruggling in portentous birth
Weep and rejoice!

Manes of th' unnumbered Slain!

Ye that gasp'd on WARSAW's plain!

Ye that erst at ISMAIL's tower,

When human [*R*]uin chok'd the streams, / r

Fell in Conquest's glutted hour

[']

Infants' *Mid Women's shrieks and Infant s' screams;

Whose shrieks, whose screams were vain to stir

Loud-laughing, red-eyed Massacre!

Spirits of th' uncoffin'd Slain,

Sudden blasts of Triumph swelling

Oft at night, in misty train

Rush around her narrow Dwelling!

Th' exterminating Fiend is fled—

(Foul her Life and dark her Doom!)

Mighty Army of the Dead,

Dance, like Death-fires, round her Tomb!

Then with prophetic song relate

Each some sceptered Murderer's fate!

[MS.] * NB Print the line thus—
Mid Women's shrieks & Infants' screams,
the ' put *after* the s' in infants'

[When shall sceptered Slaughter cease?

Awhile He crouch'd O Victor France!

Beneath the lightning of thy Lance,

With treacherous dalliance wooing Peace.

But soon up-springing from his dastard trance

The boastful, [bloody] son of Pride betrayed

His hatred of the blest and blessing Maid.

One cloud, O Freedom! cross'd thy orb of Light

And sure, he deem'd, that Orb was quench'd in
night:

For still does MADNESS *roam on* GUILT'S *bleak*
dizzy height!]

ANTISTROPHE I.

DEPARTING YEAR! 'twas on no earthly shore

My soul beheld thy Vision. Where, alone,

["With treacherous dalliance wooing peace."—*At the time this Ode was being composed, our Ambassador had returned from Paris; the French Directory professing to consider his ultimatum as an insult to the Republic.]*

[MS.] [*"One cloud, O Freedom!"—At the time our Ambassador delivered in his ultimatum, the French had received a check from the Arch-duke Charles.]*

Voiceless and stern, before the Cloudy Throne
Aye Memory sits ; there garmented with gore,
With many an unimaginable groan
Thou storiedst thy sad Hours ! Silence ensued :
Deep [*S*]ilence o'er th' etherial Multitude, / s
Whose wreathed Locks with snow-white Glories shone.
Then, his eye wild ardors glancing,
From the choired Gods advancing,
The SPIRIT of the EARTH made reverence meet,
And stood up beautiful before the Cloudy Seat!

ANTISTROPHE II.

On every Harp, on every Tongue,
While the mute Enchantment hung [:] / ;
Like Midnight from a thunder cloud ^ -
Spake the sudden SPIRIT loud—
" Thou in stormy Blackness throning
" Love and uncreated Light,

II

"By the Earth's unsolaced groaning
"Seize thy terrors, Arm of Might!
"By Belgium's corse impeded flood!
"By Vendee steaming Brother's blood!
"By PEACE with proffer'd insult scar'd,
"Masked hate and envying scorn!
"By Years of Havoc yet unborn;
"And Hunger's bosom to the frost-winds bar'd!
"But chief by Afric's wrongs
"Strange, horrible, & foul!
"By what deep Guilt belongs
"To the deaf Senate, "full of gifts and lies!"
"By Wealth's insensate laugh! By Tortures howl!
"Avenger, rise!
"For ever shall the bloody Island scowl?

" *By Belgium's corse impeded flood!* "—The Rhine.

"For aye, unbroken, shall her cruel Bow

"Shoot Famine's arrows o'er thy ravaged World?

"Hark! how wide NATURE joins her groans below—

Rise, God of Nature, rise! Ah why those Bolts unhurl'd?

EPODE II.

The voice had ceas'd, the Phantoms fled,

Yet still I gasp'd and reel'd with dread.

And ever when the dream of night

Renews the vision to my sight,

Cold sweat-damps gather on my limbs;

My Ears throb hot; my eyeballs start;

My Brain with horrid tumult swims;

Wild is the tempest of my Heart;

And my thick and struggling breath

Imitates the toil of Death!

No stranger agony confounds

The Soldier on the war-field spread,

When all foredone with toil and wounds[,]
Death-like he dozes among heaps of Dead!
(The strife is o'er, the day-light fled,
And the Night-wind clamours hoarse;
See! the startful Wretch's head
Lies pillow'd on a Brother's Corse!)

a new paragraph

O doomed to fall, enslav'd and vile,
O ALBION! O my mother Isle!
Thy valleys, fair as Eden's bowers,
Glitter green with sunny showers;
Thy grassy Uplands' gentle swells
Echo to the Bleat of Flocks;
(Those grassy Hills, those glitt'ring Dells
Proudly ramparted with rocks)
And Ocean mid his uproar wild
Speaks safety to his Island-child.
Hence for many a fearless age
Has social Quiet lov'd thy shore;

Nor ever sworded Foeman's rage

Or sack'd thy towers, or stain'd thy fields with gore.

^ ^ ^ a new para-graph

^ ^ ^ ^ ^ ^ ^

Disclaim'd of Heaven ! mad Av'rice at thy side

At coward distance, yet with kindling pride—

Safe 'mid thy herds and corn-fields thou hast stood,

And join'd the yell of Famine and of Blood.

All nations curse thee : and with eager wond'ring

Shall hear DESTRUCTION, like a vulture, scream !

Strange-eyed DESTRUCTION, who with many a dream

fires

Of central [*flames*] thro' nether seas upthund'ring

Soothes her fierce solitude ; yet, as she lies

[" Disclaim'd of Heaven !" *We have been preserved by our insular situation from suffering the actual horrors of War ourselves ; and we have shewn our gratitude to Providence for this immunity, by our eagerness to spread those horrors over other nations less happily situated.*

Of the one hundred and seven last years, fifty have been years of War.]

15

because I like lank so much better than dark myself J.C

[MS.] I cannot but think now that you gave me direction to alter this or I am unaccountably mistaken

By livid fount or roar of blazing stream,

× [*In the black chamber of a sulphur'd mount,*]

If ever to her lidless dragon eyes,

O ALBION ! thy predestin'd ruins rise,

The Fiend-hag on her perilous couch doth leap,

Mutt'ring distemper'd triumph in her charmed sleep.

Away, my soul, away !

In vain, in vain, the birds of warning sing—

And hark ! I hear the famin'd brood of prey

Flap their ^ [*dark*] pennons on the groaning wind ! ^ lank

Away, my soul, away !

I unpartaking of the evil thing,

With daily prayer, and daily toil[,] ^ &

Soliciting for food my scanty soil,

Have wail'd my country with a loud lament.

Now I recenter my immortal mind

[MS.] × That this line was to be omitted is not [*to be*] clearly expressed in your directions as I will show you. [*All the* MS. *notes on this page are in Cottle's hand.*—Ed.]

16

In the [*long*] (deep) sabbath of [*high*] (blest) self-content;

Cleans'd from the fears and anguish that bedim

God's Image, Sister of the Seraphim.

THE DARK LADIÈ.

THE STRIPLING'S WAR-SONG.

LEWTI.

[British Museum, Add. MSS. N°. 27, 902.]

THE DARK LADIÈ.

I

O leave the Lily on its stem;
O leave the Rose-bud on the spray;
O leave the Elder-bloom, [fair *dear*] Maids!
    And listen to my lay.

2

A cypress and a myrtle bough
This morn around my Harp you twin'd,
Because it fashion'd sad and sweet
    It's murmurs to the wind;

3

And now a tale of Love and Woe,
A woful tale of Love I sing:
Hark, gentle Maidens! hark—it sighs
    And trembles on the string!

4

But most, my own dear Genevieve,
It sighs and trembles most for thee!
O come, and hear what cruel wrongs
Befell the Dark Ladiè.

5

Few sorrows hath she of her own,
My Hope, my Joy, my Genevieve;
She loves me best whene'er I sing
The song*s* that make[*s*] her grieve.

[*O ever in my lonely walk*]
I feed upon that blissful hour,
we
midway on the Mount [*I stood*] [*I sate*]
When [*we two stood upon the Hill*]
Beside the ruin'd tow'r.

In lonely walk and noontide dreams
[*Each thought, each feeling of the Soul,*
All lovely sights, each tender name—
All, all are Ministers of Love,
That stir our mortal frame.]

[*stole*] [*upon*]
shine stealing oe'r scene
The Moon [*be*] [*blended*] [*on*] the [*ground*]
Had
[*And*] blended with the lights of Eve—
stood near,
And she [*was there,*] my Hope, my Joy,
My own dear Genevieve!

*

doleful
[*I play'd a soft and* [*mournful*] *air,*
I sang an old and moving story—
rude
An old [*wild*] *song, that fitted well*
The Ruin wild and hoary.

With flitting Blush and downcast eyes,
In modest melancholy grace,
The Maiden stood: perchance, I gaz'd
Too fondly on her face.—]

*

Against a grey Stone rudely carv'd,
The Statue of an armed Knight,
in
She lean'd, [*the*] melancholy mood,
[*An*] To watch'd the lingering Light.—

[*I feed upon that hour of Bliss,*] [*O ever when I walk alone,*]
O ever in my waking dreams
[*That ruddy eve, that blissful hour*] I feed upon that blissful hour
sate
When midway on the Mount I [*stood*] [*When m*]
Beside the ruin'd Tower.

9

The Moonshine stealing o'er the Scene
Had blended with the lights of Eve;
And she was there, my Hope, my Joy,
My own dear Genevieve!

[*She lean'd against a tall* [*chissel'd*] *Stone,*
The Statue of a]

10

She lean'd against an armed man,
The Statue of an armed Knight;
She stood and listen'd to my Harp
Amid the lingering light.

11

I play'd a soft and doleful air,
I sang an old and moving story—
An old rude song, that fitted well
The Ruin wild and hoary.

12

She listen'd with a flitting Blush
[*With flitting Blush & downcast eyes,*]
&
With downcast eyes [*in*] modest grace
for
[*She listen'd; [and] perchance, I gaz'd*] For well she knew I could not choose
Too fondly on her face. But gaze upon her face!

14

[*I gaz'd, and when*] I sang of Love, told her how he pin'd: & ah!
The deep, the low, the pleading Tone
With which I sang another's Love,
Interpreted my own.

15

She listen'd with a flitting Blush
With down-cast eyes & modest grace;
And
[*Yet*] she forgave me, that I gaz'd
Too fondly on her face

16

But when I sang the cruel scorn,
That craz'd this bold & lovely Knight
And how he cross'd the mountain woods,
Nor rested day nor night—

17

How sometimes from the hollow Trees
And sometimes from the darksome Shade,
And sometimes starting up at once
    In green & sunny glade

18

look'd
There came, and [*star'd*] him in the Face
An[*d*] Angel beautiful & bright,
And how he knew it was a fiend,
    And yell'd with strange affright—

R . A

19

And how unknowing what he did
He leapt amid a murderous band;
And sav'd from outrage worse than death
    The Lady of the Land—

20

And how she wept & kiss'd his knees,
And how she tended him in vain ;
And how she strove to expiate
The scorn that craz'd his Brain—

21

And how she nurs'd him in a cave— ;
And how his madness went away—
When on the yellow forest leaves
A dying man he lay—

22

His dying words—but when I reach'd
That tenderest strain of all the ditty,
My falt'ring [*trembling*] Voice & pausing Harp
Disturb'd her soul with pity.—

23

All impulses of Soul & Sense
Had thrill'd my guileless Genevieve ;
The Music & the doleful Tale,
The rich & balmy Eve ;

24

And Hopes, and Fears that kindle Hope,

An undistinguishable Throng;

And gentle wishes long subdued,

—Subdued & cherish'd long—

25

[*And*] *While* *midnight*
[While] [f] Fancy, like the [nuptial] Torch

That bends & rises in the wind,

Lit up with wild and broken lights

The Tumult of her Mind.—

26

She wept with pity & delight;

She blush'd with love & maiden shame
like the *of a dream,*
[The] And [in a] murmur [faint and sweet]
[I heard her] breathe my name]
[She half-pronounced my name]
She breathed her Lover's name—

27

I saw her gentle Bosom heave

Th' inaudible & frequent sigh;
modest
And ah! the [bashful] Maiden mark'd

The wanderings of my eye[s]—

28

side
And closely to my [heart] she press'd,
And closer still with bashful art,
[And ask'd me with her swimming eyes]
might
That I [would] rather feel than see
The swelling of her Heart
[Her gentle Bosom rise.—]

29

[And now serene, serene & chaste,] I calm'd her fears; & she was calm
[But soon in calm and solemn tone]
And
[She] told her love with maiden pride;

And so I won my Genevieve,
dear
My [bright] & lovely Bride.]

30

And now once more a tale of Woe,

A woful tale of love I sing

For thee, my Genevieve, it sighs

And trembles on the string.

31

When last I sang of Him whose heart

Was broken by a Woman's scorn—

And how he cross'd the mountain woods

All frantic & forlorn;

32

I promis'd thee a [*illeg.*] moving Tale
Of Man's perfidious cruelty—
Come then & hear what cruel wrongs
    Befell the dark Ladiè.

The Dark Ladiè.——

[*ANOTHER MS.*]

All thoughts, all passions, all delights,
All, all that stirs this mortal frame,
  All are but ministers of Love
    And fan his sacred flame.

O ever in my waking dreams
I feed upon that happy hour
  When midway on the mount I sate
    Beside the ruin'd tower.

The moonshine stealing o'er the Scene
Had blended with the lights of Eve;
  And she was there, my Hope, my Joy,
    My own dear Genevieve!

She lean'd against the armed Man,
The statue of the armed Knight;
  She stood and listen'd to my Harp
    Amid the lingering Light.

I play'd a soft and doleful air,
I sang an old and moving story ;
  And old rude song that fitted well
    The ruin wild and hoary.

She listen'd with a flitting Blush,
With downcast eyes and modest grace ;
  For well she knew I could not choose
    But gaze upon her face.

I told her of the Knight that wore
Upon his shield a burning Brand,
  And how for ten long years he woo'd
    The Lady of the Land.

[MS. ends here, in the middle of the page—the following begins on a fresh leaf—Ed.]

And Hopes, and Fears that kindle Hope,
An undistinguishable Throng,
And gentle Wishes long subdued
Subdued and cherish'd long!

She wept with pity and delight,
She blush'd with love and maiden shame;
And like the murmur of a dream
I heard her breathe my name.

I saw her Bosom heave and swell,
Heave and swell with inward sighs—
I could not chuse but love to see
Her gentle Bosom rise.

Her wet cheeks glow'd: she stepp'd aside—
As conscious of my Look she stepp'd:
Then suddenly with timorous eye,
She fled to me and wept.

She half-inclos'd me with her arms,
She prest me with a meek embrace,
And
[*Then*] bending back her head, look'd up
And gaz'd upon my face.

'Twas partly, Love & partly [*f*] Fear,
And partly twas a bashful Art,
That [*rather*] I might rather feel than see
The swelling of her Heart

I calm'd her Fears, & she was calm,
And told her Love with maiden pride;
And so I won my Genevieve,
My bright & beauteous Bride.

[MS. ends here near the top of the page.]

THE STRIPLING'S WAR-SONG.

IMITATED FROM THE GERMAN OF STOLBERG.

My noble old Warrior! this Heart has beat high
Since you told of the Deeds that our Countrymen
wrought—
Sabre, ung
Ah give me the [*Falchion*], that h[*angs*] by thy Thigh,
And I too will fight as my Forefathers fought.

O despise not my Youth/ for my Spirit is steel'd
And I know, there is strength in the grasp of my Hand:
Yea, as firm as thyself would I move to the Field
And as proudly would die for my dear Native-land!

In the sports of my Childhood I mimick'd the Fight;
Shrill
[*And t*] The [*sound*] of a Trumpet suspended my
breath;
And my fancy still wander'd by [*d*] Day and by Night
Amid tumults and perils, 'mid conquest and Death!

in the heat of my Trance
My own eager Shout [*when the Armies advance*]

How oft it awakes me from dreams full of Glory,
[*As*]
[*When*] I meant to have leapt on the Hero of France
When
And have dash'd him to earth pale and breathless and
gory !

As
[*When*] late thro' the City with bannerets streaming
[*The*] To the [*Sound*] of [*the*] Trumpets
music
[*With a terrible beauty*] the Warriors flew by:

(With helmet & scymitar naked and gleaming

On their proud trampling thunder-hoof'd Steeds did
they fly ;)

[*And the Host pacing after in gorgeous parade*

All mov'd to one measure in front and in rear ;
Pipe
And the [*Flute,*] *Drum & Trumpet such harmony made*

As the souls of the Slaughter'd would loiter to hear !]

I sped to yon Heath that is lonely & bare—
For
[*And*] each nerve
[*For my Soul*] was unquiet, each pulse in alarm!
I hurl'd my mock-lance thro' the objectless Air
And in open-ey'd Dream prov'd the strength of my
Arm.

Yes! noble old Warrior! this Heart has beat high
Since you told of the Deeds that our Countrymen
wrought:
Ah! give me the Falchion that hung by thy [*thig*]
Thigh
And I too will fight as my [*illeg.*] Forefathers fought!

S. T. COLERIDGE.

[*LEWTI;*

or, the Circassian's Love Chant.]

High o'er the silver rocks I roved
To forget the form I loved
In hopes fond fancy would be kind
And steal my Mary from my mind
  'Twas twilight & the lunar beam
Sailed slowly o'er Tamaha's stream
As down its sides the water strayed
Bright on a rock the moonbeam play'd
It shone half-sheltered from the view
By pendent boughs of tressy yew

True, true to love but false to rest,
So fancy whispered to my breast,
So shines her forehead smooth & fair
Gleaming through her sable hair
I turned to heaven—but viewed on high
The languid lustre of her eye
The moons mild radiant edge I saw
Peeping a black-arched cloud below
Nor yet its faint & paly beam
Could tinge its skirt with yellow gleam
   I saw the white waves o'er & o'er
Break against a curved shore
Now disappearing from the sight
Now twinkling regular & white
Her mouth, her smiling mouth can shew
As white & regular a row
Haste [*H*]haste, some God indulgent prove
And bear me, bear me to my love
Then might—for yet the sultry hour
Glows from the sun's oppressive power

Then might her bosom soft & white
Heave upon my swimming sight
As yon two swans together heave
Upon the gently-swelling wave
Haste—haste some God indulgent prove
And bear—oh bear me to my love